What readers are saying about In 30 Minutes guides:

Google Drive & Docs In 30 Minutes

"I bought your Google Docs guide myself (my new company uses it) and it was really handy. I loved it."

"I have been impressed by the writing style and how easy it was to get very familiar and start leveraging Google Docs. I can't wait for more titles. Nice job!"

Twitter In 30 Minutes

"A perfect introduction to Twitter. Quick and easy read with lots of photos. I finally understand the # symbol!"

"Clarified any issues and concerns I had and listed some excellent precautions."

Excel Basics In 30 Minutes

"Fast and easy. The material presented is very basic but it is also accessible with step-by-step screenshots and a friendly tone more like a friend or co-worker explaining how to use Excel than a technical manual."

"An excellent little guide. For those who already know their way around Excel, it'll be a good refresher course. Definitely plan on passing it around the office."

LinkedIn In 30 Minutes

"This book does everything it claims. It gives you a great introduction to LinkedIn and gives you tips on how to make a good profile."

"I already had a LinkedIn account, which I use on a regular basis, but still found the book very helpful. The author gave examples and explained why it is important to detail and promote your account."

Dropbox In 30 Minutes

"I was intimidated by the whole idea of storing my files in the cloud, but this book took me through the process and made it so easy."

"This was truly a 30-minute tutorial and I have mastered the basics without bugging my 20-year-old son! Yahoo!"

"Very engaging and witty."

LinkedIn

In 30 Minutes

How to create a rock-solid LinkedIn profile and build connections that matter

SECOND EDITION

Angela Rose

In 30 Minutes® Guides
QUICK GUIDES FOR A COMPLEX WORLD®
in30minutes.com

LinkedIn In 30 Minutes
Second Edition
ISBN: 978-1-939924-52-0
Library of Congress Control Number: 2015916480
Copyright © 2016 by i30 Media Corporation.

Original interior design *by* Monica Thomas for TLC Graphics, www.TLCGraphics.com. Interior design assisted and composition *by* Rick Soldin, book-comp.com.

Contents

Introduction

I'm going to let you in on a little secret: I haven't always been on LinkedIn. In fact, I wasn't even aware the professional networking platform existed until 2006.

At the time, I was working as a manager in the creative department of a small marketing company. Our clients were primarily in the mortgage and real estate industries. They would personalize the postcards and newsletters my team and I had created with their logos and contact information before mailing them to their databases. One day a real estate agent asked us to include the web address (or URL) for his LinkedIn profile.

I was intrigued. While I was not a social media newbie—I posted hilarious, adorable and poignant pictures of my cats on Facebook almost every day—the concept of social network for professional people was different. I checked out the agent's profile, took a quick tour of LinkedIn's features, and left it at that. I had a job I loved. I was going to work there until I died. I didn't need what LinkedIn had to offer.

Then the housing bubble burst, causing property values to plummet and thousands of homeowners to default on their mortgages. No one could buy, and no one could sell. Our client base began to contract. As we put raises on hold and closed our offices on Fridays, I had to face an unpleasant reality: It was very possible I'd need to find a new job—or strike out on my own—in the near future.

Suddenly, being on LinkedIn looked like a really good idea. I spent 30 minutes that first Friday setting up a free profile. While I only filled out the basics, I felt better having done something that might help me if the unthinkable happened. About one year later, it did. By then I had built the foundations of a freelance writing and editing business. I had more than a dozen regular clients, and their assignments were enough, along with some savings, to ensure I would be able to keep paying my bills (and feeding those cats) as I continued to grow The Quirky Creative.

LinkedIn helped me make it happen. I made a habit of connecting with the decision-makers at every company that used my services. This kept me front of mind, and resulted in referrals and repeat assignments. I asked for—and gave—recommendations, then shared the glowing endorsements with potential clients. This helped me to land more assignments. I added a professional photo, packed my background summary with keywords and personality, and uploaded clips from my growing portfolio of published work.

With every enhancement, my profile received more views. I received more emails from professionals and companies interested in the services I provided. I landed more assignments, and I was able to maintain the lifestyle to which my cats were accustomed (i.e. gourmet kibble, frequent catnip binges and all the toy mice they could shove under the sofa).

In fact, LinkedIn actually led to the book you are reading today. The publisher of In 30 Minutes guides found my profile, liked the contents, and offered me the opportunity to share what I have learned about using this increasingly important social media platform with all of you—no cat photos required!

Not just an online resume

As the above anecdote illustrates, LinkedIn is more than just an online catalog of former employers and responsibilities. It's a tool that can have a significant and positive impact on your life, whether you use it to search for a new job, network with other professionals in your industry, establish an online presence or even learn more about potential vendors and service providers (I used it to 'vet' my cats' veterinarian).

Consider the following numbers:

➤ LinkedIn has approximately 400 million members, located in practically every country in the world. Whether you want to connect with a former supervisor, a colleague you met at a conference, the recruiter at your dream company, or even your old high school track coach (go Warriors!), you are likely to find them on LinkedIn.

➤ According to a recent LinkedIn report, the network hosts more than 3 million active job listings. Advertised positions are in dozens of industries ranging from agriculture and construction to finance and healthcare. Whatever your area of expertise, you are likely to find employment opportunities on LinkedIn.

➤ A 2014 Jobvite Social Recruiting Survey found that 93% of recruiters use or plan to use social media platforms to fill jobs. Among these recruiters, 94% use LinkedIn. Whether you are actively searching for a new job or are a passive candidate—defined as interested in opportunities though not active in the job search—joining LinkedIn will make it easier for employers to find you.

How are people leveraging LinkedIn?

While students and recent college grads are the fastest growing demographic on LinkedIn, the social media network has more than 80 million members between the ages of 30 and 49, and more than 100 million who are 50 years of age or older.

How are they using their profiles? Here are just a few examples:

➤ **Duane is an account rep for a manufacturer of construction equipment.** A frequent trade show attendee, he uses LinkedIn to learn more about the professionals he plans to network with on his trips… and later uses LinkedIn to maintain connections afterward. This has helped him land new accounts as well as forge relationships that may prove valuable when it's time to take the next step in his career.

➤ **Samantha is a recent college graduate with a degree in human resources management.** She is currently interviewing for jobs as a payroll administrator, and she uses LinkedIn to learn more about the companies she is visiting as well as the professionals conducting the interviews. Thanks to the keywords in her profile, she has been approached by a number of recruiters for jobs she otherwise wouldn't have heard about.

➤ **John is a freelance graphic designer.** While he hasn't had a regular 9-to-5 job in the last decade, he has used the experience section of his LinkedIn profile to feature several of his current and former contract projects. With dozens of recommendations and hundreds of endorsements, his profile enhances his professional reputation.

➤ **Amanda was laid off in December, and she has been using LinkedIn to search for a new job in the healthcare industry.** A registered nurse, she has connected with the hiring managers at several local hospitals using InMail. She is a member of a half-dozen nursing- and healthcare-related groups and regularly participates in discussions to increase her visibility. She has also spent time enhancing her LinkedIn profile with a current, professional photo and keywords to improve her search ranking.

➤ **Robert is a retired fireman.** He's not interested in going back to work full-time, or even part-time for that matter, but he likes to see what former colleagues are doing and stay current on the latest industry news. He uses LinkedIn to connect with other public safety professionals, learn new information about the field, and share his experience and opinions with the members of related discussion groups.

Are you ready to get started?

Whatever your age, profession, or employment status, you are almost certain to benefit from learning to use LinkedIn—and doing so is surprisingly easy. It doesn't matter if you are a complete newbie or a frequent social media consumer, this guide will show you how to navigate the LinkedIn platform, register for a free account, set up your profile step-by-step, connect with other members, join discussion groups and search for jobs—all in the time it would take to watch a dozen YouTube cat videos. We only have 30 minutes, so let's get started!

CHAPTER 1

A brief tour of LinkedIn

Robert McDonald commented on this. Joe DeVito shared that. NBC Universal needs a newsroom assistant. Debbie Lee has a new connection. Don't miss this story on how to make a cat fort out of nothing but recycled water bottles and duct tape...

I must admit, the first few times I logged in and visited my LinkedIn homepage, I was more than a little overwhelmed by the variety of information displayed on the screen. I hadn't signed up to learn how to make a cat fort—though I'd find that sort of instruction interesting under other circumstances. No, I was there to establish a professional online presence and connect with people who could help me should I eventually need a new job. It was obvious that I was going to have to devote some time to figuring out how to do it.

Fortunately, you don't have to puzzle out LinkedIn's user interface alone. Not only has the company dramatically simplified it in recent years, but I'm here to talk you through everything you will find on your homepage and profile, from the toolbar icons and newsfeed to how many people have recently viewed your information.

Understanding toolbar links and icons

As in most software programs, LinkedIn's *toolbar* runs across the top of the browser window. The toolbar links are always the same—whether you are viewing your homepage, your profile, another user's profile or any other LinkedIn pages such as discussion groups, search results or LinkedIn Pulse. Here is a brief description of the icons and links as well as where they'll take you:

➤ **Home**: You can think of the home link as your own pair of magic ruby slippers. Click on it, and you will find yourself instantly transported back to your LinkedIn homepage. The LinkedIn logo located above the home link in the toolbar also serves this purpose.

➤ **Profile**: This link takes you to your profile page. It includes a dropdown menu with the options *Edit Your Profile*, *Who's Viewed Your Profile*, and *Your Updates*. Select the first option to make additions or changes to your profile page. Use the second for data on visitors to your profile page in the last 90 days as well as how you rank for profile views. The third will display recent activity on the website, including updates you have liked and posts you have shared.

➤ **My Network**: Select *Connections* from the dropdown menu to see a list of the professionals in your LinkedIn network. *Add Contacts* gives the option to import your address book from a number of email platforms. This can make it easier to find people you already know in real life. Choose *People You May Know* to have LinkedIn's algorithms suggest new connections for you to make. The *Find Alumni* link will take you to a page where you can search for professionals on the site based on the university they attended.

➤ **Jobs**: If you are on LinkedIn to find your next position, click this link to visit the jobs page where you can search for opportunities by job title, company name, location, industry, function, and salary.

➤ **Interests**: Choose from the dropdown menu under *Interests* to navigate quickly to other LinkedIn content you may find interesting. Choose *Companies* to follow, review posts and discussions taking place in your Groups, read LinkedIn user content published in *Pulse*, find a *University* where you can continue your education, check out *SlideShare* slideshows on thousands of topics, or browse LinkedIn's *Online Learning* library.

> **Business Services**: Unless you are on LinkedIn to recruit employ-ees—or want to pay to advertise your own services—you are unlikely to need to visit any of the business services dropdown links. Options include *Post a Job*, *Talent Solutions*, *Advertise* and *Sales Solutions*.

> **Premium**: LinkedIn memberships come in free and premium variet-ies. In this book, we are mainly going to focus on using the social media network with a free profile. However, you may want to look into the benefits of a paid LinkedIn account if you plan to apply for a lot of jobs, want to aggressively grow your network of connections, are looking for sales leads, or need to hire your own employees.

> **Search**: Type a name or keyword (such as a job title or location) into the search field, click on the blue magnifying glass icon, and LinkedIn will return a list of relevant results. To focus the search, use the drop-down menu on the left side of the field to narrow the search to People, Companies, Universities, and more. Click the *Advanced* link to focus the search even more.

To the right of the search field are several icons:

> **Messages**: The chat bubble icon will show your most recent LinkedIn messages from other members. You can configure LinkedIn to forward messages to your real email inbox, as described in Chapter 2.

> **Notifications**: Click on the flag to see a list of endorsements you have received, new members you might know, and posts published by pro-fessionals in your network.

> **Grow My Network**: In case you haven't figured this out by now, LinkedIn really wants you to expand your network. The silhouette icon is another way for you to navigate to pending invitations and suggested connections, as well as an interface for uploading your email addresses to LinkedIn.

➤ **Account and Settings**: The miniature version of your LinkedIn profile photo in the toolbar has a dropdown menu to sign out of your account, upgrade to a premium membership, change your profile language, manage job postings and company pages, and adjust privacy and other settings. We will look into account settings in more detail in the next chapter.

Your custom LinkedIn homepage

Each time you sign into your account, the LinkedIn homepage is the first thing you will see. Unlike your profile—which is all about you and visible to the public—the homepage is where you go to find out what's going on in your network. It's also gives a snapshot of how your profile and updates are doing within the LinkedIn universe.

The top portion of the LinkedIn homepage is known as the *dashboard*. It was designed to give you quick feedback on how your profile and updates are performing, as well as make it easy for you to perform common LinkedIn actions. When you look at my homepage dashboard above, you will see my picture, a link to the profile editing page and a couple of interesting details.

At a glance, we can see that six people have viewed my profile in the past 30 days. An update I shared—a link to one of my recently published articles—has received 10 views.

If I want to *Share an update*, *Upload a photo* or *Publish a post*, I can do so by clicking the appropriate link on the dashboard. I can also maintain contact with professionals in my network using the *Ways to keep in touch* feature. LinkedIn has identified two events that currently warrant action. I can address a particular item by liking or commenting, or skipping it altogether.

Beneath the dashboard on the homepage is the network updates feed. Click on the three-dot icon in the right-hand corner to sort the posts by *Top updates* or *Recent updates*. Within this feed, you will find articles, photos and other content your connections have shared or liked. You will also see updates they have made to their profiles (unless they have adjusted their settings to hide updates—more on that later) and their newest connections. LinkedIn likes to throw a few suggestions into the mix as well. You will find both people you may know as well as jobs that may interest you.

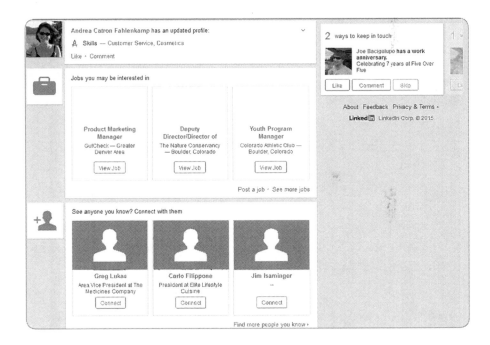

Your LinkedIn profile

We have now arrived at everyone's favorite part of LinkedIn—the profile page. It's all about you: your background, job history, education, interests, and whatever else you may want to share with other LinkedIn members. They can see most of your profile (except details like your email, phone number, and address) when they search your name or click your name in an update or a group. They can see all of your profile if they connect with you.

You can view your own profile page by clicking the *Profile* link in the toolbar or the *Improve your profile* link in your homepage dashboard. We are going to dig into profile components in great detail in later chapters. However, here is a quick overview of the basic pieces using the profile of Ken Gagne, a Boston-area Internet specialist, as an example.

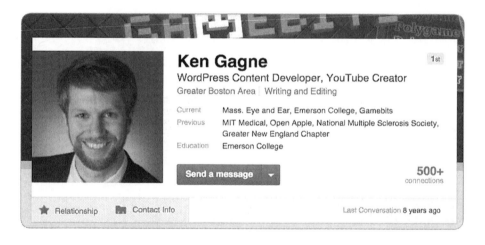

➤ **General Information**: We can think of the top portion of the LinkedIn profile as a virtual business card. It contains the person's name, location, industry, and current employer as well as snippets of his or her job and education history. Clicking on *Contact Info*, visitors will see that person's LinkedIn URL and email address.

Protip: The header can also contain a professional headline. As I explain in Chapter 3, it's something I recommend you include in yours.

Background

 Summary

Currently a web producer in the healthcare industry, adjunct faculty member in the publishing field, game industry multimedia content producer, talk show podcaster, volunteer non-profits webmaster, and retrocomputing enthusiast. I've also been a beat reporter, newspaper layout designer, magazine editor, tech writer, high school English teacher, online community moderator, and entertainment blogger.

 Experience

Multimedia Communications Producer
Mass. Eye and Ear
October 2015 – Present (2 months) | Boston, MA

Develop and execute online strategy, including editorial responsibility for website and all social media platforms, for Massachusetts Eye and Ear Infirmary, ranked #1 by U.S. News & World Report for ENT and eye care. Includes content development and management, daily CMS oversight/troubleshooting, and production of email newsletters, videos, and audio podcasts.

Adjunct Faculty
Emerson College

➤ **Background**: We can think of the *Background* portion of the LinkedIn profile as a virtual resume—though it can be much more robust than anything printed on paper. It contains your previous employment experience—with associated recommendations—projects you have worked on, volunteer experience, skills, publications, education, honors, and awards.

For example, a quick scan of Ken's background reveals he is currently working as a multimedia producer for Massachusetts Eye & Ear Infirmary, and is also an adjunct faculty member at Emerson College in Boston. Scrolling down, he has many other positions listed, including previous jobs and volunteer activities.

Note: Ken had the option to include paragraph or two in the *Summary* section above his work background. He didn't choose to do so, but it's something I'd recommend you include within yours. The summary section is a great place for keywords, which can help people and employers find you. This is discussed in more detail later.

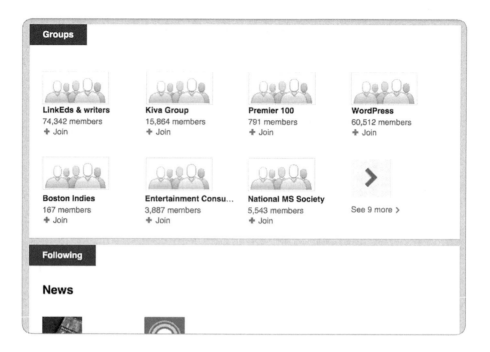

➤ **Groups and Following**: At the bottom of your LinkedIn profile, viewers will find more information about the groups you belong to as well
as various news subjects and organizations you follow on the social
media network. We can see that Ken is a member of more than a dozen
groups on LinkedIn. Under the Following tab, there is a long list of
news items, companies, and causes that Ken is interested in.

LinkedIn apps overview

In addition to the website, LinkedIn offers members a suite of mobile apps to make it easy for you to build your network, search for jobs and enjoy LinkedIn content on the go. In this book, we are focusing on how to use LinkedIn from your desktop or laptop browser. However, you may want to download and explore LinkedIn for Phone, LinkedIn for iPad, LinkedIn Job Search and/or LinkedIn Pulse later on. The apps are not as full-featured as the LinkedIn website, but they offer ways to quickly access your LinkedIn network and browse content and jobs on LinkedIn.

CHAPTER 2

Registration

Now that you have an idea of what to expect and how to get around once you are on LinkedIn, you are ready for the next step: registering for an account. Doing so takes just a few minutes. Once you have completed the registration process, we will move on to setting up a basic profile (Chapter 3) and then learn more about what is needed to ensure you have maximized its effectiveness (chapters 4, 5, and 6).

How to register online

Open your web browser and type *linkedin.com* into the address bar. You should now see something like this:

To create your LinkedIn account, you will need to enter your first name, last name, email, and a password with six or more characters. You will use your email address and password to log into LinkedIn in the future. LinkedIn will use your email address to confirm your account during the registration process and send you notifications and other messages later on.

> **Protip:** Your email address will also become part of your LinkedIn profile. While it is possible to change it at any time, you can simplify things by using a professional email address now. You probably wouldn't want to put catlover86@aol.com on your resume, so it makes sense to keep it off your LinkedIn profile as well. If you don't have a business-appropriate email address to use, or don't want to use your employer's email domain, consider setting up a free Gmail account at gmail.com.

After you enter the required data in the corresponding fields and click the *Join Now* button, you will be brought to a form asking for basic information:

Let's start with your profile
This will set you up for success on LinkedIn

Country *
United States

ZIP code (e.g. 94043) *
80504

Are you a student? *   Yes   • No

Job title *
Executive Assistant

Company *
The Quirky Creative

Industry *
Writing & Editing

Create your profile   * Required information

Your LinkedIn profile is key to everything you do on the website. Without a profile, you cannot make connections, search for jobs, or join groups. For this reason, LinkedIn wants to start filling in information on your profile right now—beginning with your country, zip code, job title, company, and industry. LinkedIn will use this information to suggest potential employers, people to connect with, and essays by thought leaders in your industry or field. Enter the required information, click *Create your profile* and you will be asked about what you intend to use LinkedIn for:

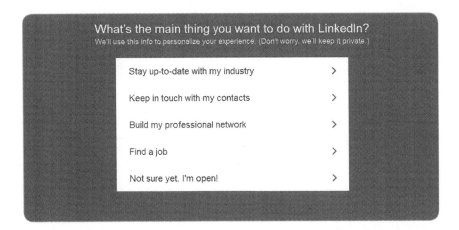

Jezebel Kitten, my executive assistant, doesn't know what she wants to use LinkedIn for, so she is going to select *Not sure yet. I'm open!*

The next step involves importing your email address book. Doing so will enable you to find some of the professionals you already know on LinkedIn without the need to search for them. According to LinkedIn's privacy policy, they will only use the data within your address book to manage and leverage your contacts who are LinkedIn members and help you grow your network by suggesting professionals you may know but are not yet connected to on the website.

You can remove uploaded address data whenever you like. However, because connecting an address book is not necessary for registration—and Jezebel Kitten does not have an address book—we are going to click *Skip*. At this point, you have to confirm your email account to continue. LinkedIn has sent a confirmation email to Jezebel Kitten at the address she entered when beginning the registration process. Once she gets that email and clicks on the confirmation link, she'll wind up at a screen that looks something like this:

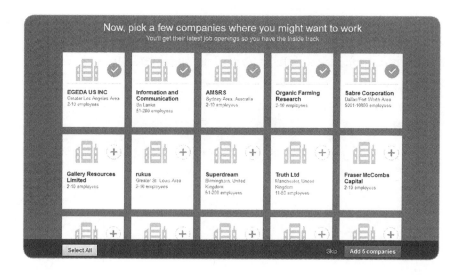

If you are looking for a new job, or think you might want to do so in the future, you can select companies that interest you on this page. If you are not planning a job search—or don't see any companies that you find appealing—you can click *Skip*.

At this point, LinkedIn's algorithms kick in and suggest jobs that might be a good fit:

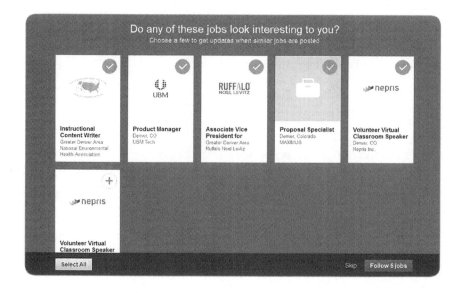

If you would like to see updates on your homepage network feed when companies post similar jobs, you can select a few to follow. Otherwise, choose *Skip* and move on. After being prompted to try out LinkedIn's mobile apps, you're done!

Congratulations! You now have an account and can begin connecting with other professionals, joining groups, participating in discussions, searching for jobs, posting updates, uploading photos and presentations, and more.

But before you start doing so, you should really spend a few minutes filling in the rest of the basic information on your profile. Think of it like getting dressed: You wouldn't leave the house without your clothing and shoes, would you? Nor should you start your LinkedIn journey with a naked profile:

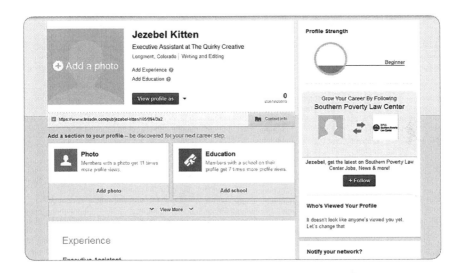

How to make your LinkedIn profile stand out

The more complete your LinkedIn profile is, the better it will perform. In fact, according to LinkedIn data, users with complete profiles are 40 times more likely to been seen by other members. More views generally equate to more opportunities—whether you are looking for a new job, establishing yourself as an expert in your industry, or using the network to market your services.

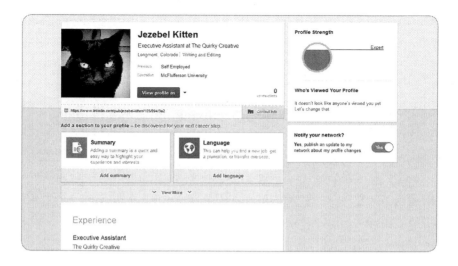

You will find a helpful *Profile Strength* meter in the upper right-hand corner of your new profile page. As you can see, Jezebel Kitten's profile is currently rated *beginner*. Yours will be as well—at least until you add a few essentials. LinkedIn will not consider your profile *complete* until it includes:

➤ Your location and industry

➤ Your current position (plus a description)

➤ Two past positions

➤ Your education details

➤ At least three skills

➤ A profile photo

➤ At least 50 connections

Most people don't complete their profile on the first try. For some, it may take months of adding connections to reach that level. And while it's a wise goal to strive for (especially if you want to make the most of your time on the network) you can still improve your profile ranking by entering some of the information in the list above.

As you can see, Jezebel Kitten was able to reach the *expert* profile level quite easily. It took her less than 15 minutes to upload a profile image and add details about her current and previous job:

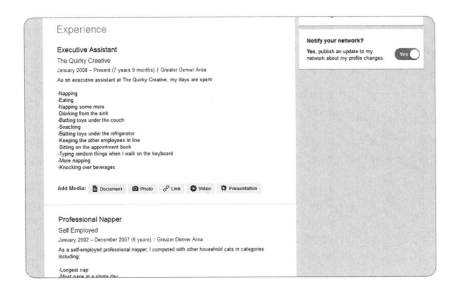

Later her profile is updated to include a university, as well as skills:

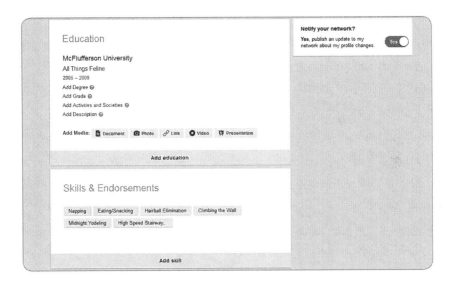

Though it would actually be impossible for a cat to do this (at least by her-self) LinkedIn's profile editing interface is so intuitive, even newbies should find it a breeze to operate.

For example, to add a photo, all you need to do is click on the photo box and then follow the instructions in the upload wizard. To add your work experience, click the *Add Experience* link in your profile header or the *Add a position* link at the bottom of the experience box. Adding your education and skills is as simple as selecting the corresponding box beneath *Add a section to your profile*, and then entering information in the fields provided.

Once you have the basics covered, you can begin reaching out to other LinkedIn members, joining groups, and building your network of contacts. You can also continue improving your profile by adding other information you would like LinkedIn users to know about you. There is no limit to the number of changes you can make or when you can make them. I'm still tweaking my LinkedIn profile to this day.

Five Privacy & Settings options you should change right now

Maybe you are not ready to take your LinkedIn profile public just yet. Per-haps you have decided you want to add another email or a phone number to your account. You may even want to change your password at some point—and you will do all of this by selecting *Privacy and Settings* under the Account and Settings icon (the miniature version of your LinkedIn profile photo) on the LinkedIn toolbar.

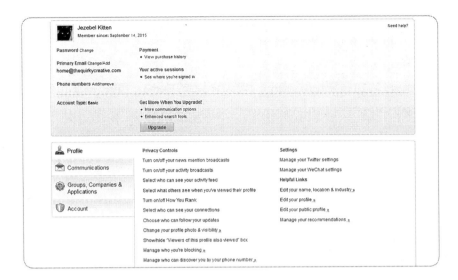

As you can see, there is a lot you can do from this page. Feel free to explore your options by clicking on any of the links displayed on the *Profile*, *Communications*, *Groups, Companies & Applications* and *Account* tabs. Here are five that you should consider changing right away:

1. **Profile: Turn on/off activity broadcasts –** If you would rather not fill your connections' network feeds with updates every time you make a profile change, you should uncheck the box for broadcasting profile activity. You can also do this by flipping the toggle in the *Notify your network?* checkbox on the profile editing page.

2. **Profile: Select who can see your activity feed –** The default setting is *Your connections*, but if you would prefer to keep new connections, likes, and comments made on other members' posts private, set this to *Only you*.

3. **Profile: Edit your public profile –** Click on this link, and you will be brought to your public profile page. On the right-hand side, you will see options for who can view your public profile. If you would rather keep your work-in-progress under wraps for now, select *Make my public profile visible to no one*. This will prevent your profile from becoming searchable on the web.

Note: Even if you are hidden to people using Google or other search engines, other LinkedIn members who search for you on the site will still be able to view your profile—all the more reason to make it great!

4. **Communications: Set the frequency of emails –** If LinkedIn is sending you too many email messages, you can change your email settings. While most people want to be notified when they have received an endorsement or a message from another user, group notifications and marketing from LinkedIn can overwhelm your inbox.

5. **Account: Manage advertising preferences –** LinkedIn—like every other social media network—likes to know what you have been doing online. If you don't want them to track your web browsing activities and show you targeted ads, you can change this setting here.

Protip: Turning off your activity broadcasts is a wise move if you are currently employed and do not want your coworkers or employer to know that you are looking for a new job. Updating your profile may be seen as an indication that you are planning to change companies.

CHAPTER 3

Making your profile great

A LinkedIn profile can be a powerful tool to help you achieve your professional goals, from taking the next step in your career or building a network of prospective clients to strengthening your web presence or growing your influence. However, its power is only as great as the time and effort you put into it. Setting up the basics is enough to get you started. But truly maximizing your profile's potential—and the number of opportunities it's likely to generate for you—requires a bit more effort.

In this chapter, we are going to dig deeper into the critical elements that should be part of every great LinkedIn profile. I will list some best practices for the most important sections. Less essential profile sections you may be able to skip entirely.

Also note that you do not have to tackle everything at once. A top-notch LinkedIn profile takes some time to perfect. The important thing to remember is that you are already well on your way.

The 9 most critical elements of your profile

Want a comprehensive LinkedIn profile that impresses every member who views it? Of course you do! And you can have one—if you make sure you include these nine critical elements.

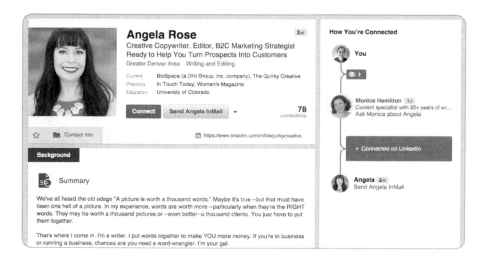

#1 Use a photo, and make it great: Online, as in real life, we make instantaneous judgments about every image we see. And the first thing most people notice when viewing a LinkedIn profile is the photo. It shapes their initial impression, subtly influencing their reaction to everything else on the profile. Include a photo and your profile will get more views—14 percent more, according to data from LinkedIn.

For this reason, LinkedIn is not the place for casual snapshots from your birthday or your last vacation—no matter how epic they may have been. You need a professional photo if you want to ensure you are taken seriously by recruiters or other professionals who view your profile page.

This doesn't mean you have to hire a paid photographer to get results. You can enlist the help of a friend with a mobile phone and still end up with a perfectly suitable photo if you remember these best practices:

➤ Take the photo in a well-lit area; natural light from a window is always preferable to that generated by the flash.

➤ Avoid distracting backgrounds.

➤ Ask your friend to step in close so your head and shoulders fill the frame.

➤ Don't forget a relaxed smile. Research has shown that we perceive happy faces as more trustworthy.

➤ Finally, dress appropriately. If your career requires formal attire, wear a suit. If it allows creative latitude, you can go with business-casual clothing. Check out the profiles of other professionals with your job title to see what they are wearing.

> **Protip:** It's important to update your profile photo regularly. If you connect with someone on Linked in and later meet them in real life, they are going to question your credibility if you no longer resemble your photo. Take a new one every two years or whenever you dramatically change your hairstyle or gain/lose a significant amount of weight.

#2 Add a custom headline: When you begin setting up your basic profile, LinkedIn will automatically populate the headline field with your current job title and employer. Most professionals leave it that way—but you really shouldn't. Instead, customize it to feature skills that set you apart from your competition, use it to highlight what you do, what you want to do, or a combination of the three.

For example, when I set up my LinkedIn profile, the headline defaulted to "Founder and 24-7 Word Wrangler at The Quirky Creative." That's not too bad, but I chose to change it to "Creative Copywriter, Editor, B2C Marketing Strategist Ready to Help You Turn Prospects Into Customers." This is the headline that appears in search results, which gives LinkedIn members who view my profile a better idea of the services I provide and why they might want to hire me for their projects.

Keep the following best practices in mind when writing your profile headline:

➤ You have 120 characters to use; make the most of them.

➤ While creativity is acceptable—and memorable—avoid ambiguity. For example, don't include a nonstandard job title that sounds catchy but is difficult to decipher ("Cubicle Magician Extraordinaire").

➤ Avoid words that may come across as cheesy or meaningless. These include "Superstar," "Rock Star," "Magical" and "Visionary."

➤ Avoid obscure acronyms unless they are well-known in your industry.

If writing a headline is difficult, you can ask LinkedIn to show you some examples. In edit mode, click the icon to edit your headline and a box will appear offering you the opportunity to see examples from your industry.

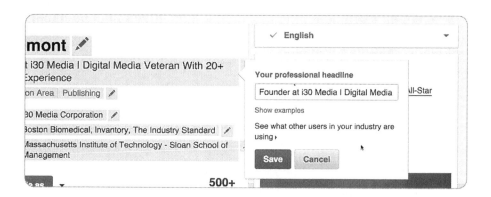

Protip: Keywords are essential in your headline (and the rest of your profile). Why? Because they influence search results and suggestion boxes. Under LinkedIn's indexing system, the headline is the highest rated field after your name. Using the right keywords within it will help recruiters and others searching for professionals like you to find your profile. The keywords you choose may include the standard title for the job you have or the job you want, your skills, certifications and services you provide. In my case, I used the keywords "copywriter," "editor," and "marketing strategist." A software engineer might include "agile," "C++" and "mobile." A nurse, a construction engineer, or a manager of a movie theater would have different sets of keywords.

#3 Include your location and industry: If you didn't leave any fields blank when registering for your LinkedIn account, this portion of your profile has already been populated. That's great news, as LinkedIn data shows that including your industry can result in 15 times more profile views.

Additionally, recruiters and professionals searching for services may narrow their search by location. Both fields become handy keywords within your profile.

#4 List your contact information: Your email address, phone number, and physical address are only visible to your connections. While you have to include an email to register a LinkedIn account, it's really up to you whether you want to include the rest of your contact information. Of course, a phone number can make it easier for recruiters to contact you if you are looking for a job. Many people leave a contact number and email address in the Summary section of their profiles.

> **Protip:** One best practice to consider is adding a link to your professional website. This is particularly important if you are in a field where a potential employer or client may want to review a portfolio of your work or take a closer look at the services or products you offer. Any website link you add will be visible to everyone on LinkedIn when viewing your profile.

#5 Create a custom LinkedIn URL: When you registered, LinkedIn automatically generated a profile URL that you can include in an email signature, resume, or even add to your business card. While these assigned URLs tend to be long and hard to remember ("linkedin.com/in/sarah-green-0a840b14"), it's possible to create a custom LinkedIn URL. Many members leave theirs as is, but if you plan to publicize your profile in any way—say, on a resume, your website, or in your email signature line—it makes sense to change it to something more memorable than a URL containing random numbers and letters.

Keep in mind these best practices when choosing a new LinkedIn URL:

➤ Your full name is generally an ideal choice. However, if it's a common name and already taken, you may need to add your middle initial or middle name as well.

➤ Adding your job title instead of your middle name is another option.

➤ If you are running your own business, you may be able to use your company name.

➤ The customizable portion of the URL can be a combination of five to 30 letters and numbers long.

#6 Add a summary: Remember those keywords I mentioned earlier? The summary section of your LinkedIn profile is another natural place to include them. However, many professionals don't even bother to include a summary. Instead, they expect viewers to scroll through everything else on their profile to get an idea of their experience and aspirations. This is a mistake. Recruiters spend mere moments scanning resumes. They—and any other busy professionals—are unlikely to spend more valuable time reviewing your entire profile unless you give them a reason to do so. Your summary can become that reason.

Background

 Summary

I am the founder of i30 Media Corporation, which publishes In 30 Minutes® guides. My passion is creating media products that empower people and improve their lives. I love working with great teams to develop cool, innovative products, and successfully bring them to market. Friends and colleagues know that I value hard work, honesty, and creativity. I am always eager to dive into the next challenge and learn from the people around me to find the best way forward.

My media career has spanned more than 20 years across three continents, including a stint in the British music industry and a six-year residence in Taipei, where I learned Mandarin and worked for a local TV network and newspaper. Returning to the Boston area, I shifted my career into the digital media world, building websites for Harvard University, developing online services for technology publisher IDG, and serving as managing editor of The Industry Standard blog platform and prediction market. Later, I founded two ventures, including a mobile software startup and i30 Media.

Company website: http://in30minutes.com

Contact: ian@in30minutes.com

Consider these best practices for writing a captivating summary:

➤ Describe your most valuable skills, notable qualifications, prior experience, and future career aspirations.

➤ Bullet points are great; they get your point across quickly.

➤ Full paragraphs will allow you to show some personality.

➤ Strive for two to three paragraphs and one bulleted list.

➤ Write in the first person and use a conversational tone.

➤ Make sure your summary is at least 40 words long. According to LinkedIn data, this will increase your odds of turning up in a search.

➤ You can use a total of 2,000 characters.

➤ Don't forget to work in those keywords!

#7 Job experience needs to be brief while reflecting accomplishments: The experience section may look like a resume, but you can do a lot more with it than you can with words printed on paper. For instance, if a company or organization you have worked for is already in LinkedIn's system, you can create a link to it from the heading of that job description.

That said, many of the same basic principles you would follow to write a resume will work on LinkedIn as well. At a minimum, you should include a job title, company name, and employment dates for each position on your LinkedIn profile. These should match your resume, or anyone comparing the two may question your credibility. Adding a description for each position is also critical. Keep the following best practices in mind when doing so:

➤ Start with a two- or three-sentence summary of your duties and your most notable accomplishments.

➤ Use a conversational tone and plenty of active verbs to ensure lively text.

➤ Whenever possible, quantify your statements with numbers—"increased sales n%," "expanded the team by hiring x full-time associates," etc.

➤ Bulleted lists are helpful, particularly when listing skills, areas of expertise, and specialties.

➤ Keep lists short; aim for between five and 10 points.

➤ Work in your keywords!

Administrative Assistant, Youth Worker
Greek Orthodox Metropolis of Boston
September 2004 – February 2008 (3 years 6 months) | Brookline, Massachusetts

- Spearheaded youth programs for greater New England within the Metropolis of Boston
- Planned and prepared for annual mission trips to third-world countries
- Coordinated business meetings and presentations
- Developed innovative marketing approaches and materials
- Fielded telephone calls and visitors

Program Director
St. Methodios Faith and Heritage Center/MBC
June 2004 – August 2007 (3 years 3 months)

- Established policies, procedures and guidelines for all programs
- Evaluated programs and provided feedback as needed
- Communicated program status and plans with Youth Director on weekly basis

---

Protip: If you have had a long career, or have changed industries at some point, you don't need to include every previous position in your profile. Much like on your print resume, you can generally limit your experience to the roles you have held in the last decade.

#8 Where did you go to school? According to LinkedIn, members who include education on their profiles get 10 times more views than those who don't. Within this section, you can note the name of each school you have attended, the dates, and your field of study, degree, grades, activities, and societies. You can even include a description of your educational experience. The name of the school is the only required field.

Boston College
Information Technology
2000 – 2002

Undergraduate-level coursework in information technology at the Woods College of Advancing Studies, Boston College.

Taipei Language Institute, China Language Institute
Mandarin
1993 – 1999

Attended TLI from 1993 to 1994 and again in 1999. Attended CLI in 1995.

Boston University
BS, Broadcasting and Film
1987 – 1991

Activities and Societies: London Internship Program

Protip: If you attended college but didn't complete your degree, you can still list the name of the university, your dates of attendance and your field of study. If you have earned more than one degree, or attended more than one school, include it on your profile in reverse order with the most recent first. Your highest level of education should always appear at the top.

#9 Add some skills: Did you complete the basic profile setup steps in the last chapter? If so, then you have already added at least three skills to your LinkedIn profile. This is great, because according to LinkedIn data, members who include skills receive 13 times more profile views than those who don't. This is because recruiters often include skills as keywords when searching for professionals.

To get the most out of this portion of your profile, keep these best practices in mind:

➤ You can add up to 50 skills, but it's best to focus on a few that are most relevant to your current career or the career you want to have in the future.

➤ By default, LinkedIn will list your most endorsed skills at the top of your list. We'll talk about endorsements later in the chapter. However, you can reorder them any time you want by clicking *Add skill* and then dragging each one to its new location.

➤ If someone recommends you for a skill that you do not want to highlight, you can remove it. In edit profile mode, click the edit icon in the skills area and then click "X" to remove unwanted skills.

Six elements to add (if you have enough time)

If you have filled out all the LinkedIn fields and sections listed above, your profile is already starting to shine. At this point, you have increased your chances of showing up in searches substantially while giving your profile viewers a comprehensive picture of who you are, what you have done, and what you would like to do in the future.

But you don't have to stop here. You may also want to add content to these less important (but still useful) LinkedIn profile sections:

1. **Volunteering Experience:** When it comes to getting the attention of recruiters, volunteer work can be nearly as important as paid work experience, particularly if it relates to your industry. You may also

want to highlight volunteer accomplishments if you are returning to the workforce after raising children or enjoying a period of retirement.

2. **Honors and Awards:** Honors and awards can set you apart from your competition, providing you are including career-related accolades. Recruiters and potential network connections may not be as impressed with recognition you for personal interests or accomplishments, such as running a half-marathon, winning a five-alarm chili contest, or taking home the bronze at an international cat show.

3. **Certifications:** If you work in an industry where certifications are valued, include those that you have earned. They can function as keywords and may be searched for by recruiters.

4. **Organizations:** If you belong to any organizations that are related to your current or future career, you can note them in this section of your LinkedIn profile.

5. **Projects:** Showcasing projects you have worked on is a nice way to show recruiters and other LinkedIn members your capabilities. Whether you are a graphic artist, writer, or consultant, consider adding projects to your profile. You can even link them to relevant positions in the experience section.

6. **Publications:** Has your work been published in a newspaper, magazine, journal, or online publication? If so, you can showcase it by adding this section to your profile.

Six sections you can skip or save for later

Believe it or not, there are still more opportunities to personalize your LinkedIn profile. While it's perfectly acceptable to skip these sections (doing so is unlikely to hurt your profile views), adding them may give other LinkedIn members an even more complete picture of you. You can learn more about each of these by clicking on the corresponding box while editing your LinkedIn profile:

1. Background photo
2. Causes you care about

3. Courses

4. Interests

5. Test scores

6. Volunteering opportunities

How to leverage endorsements for specific skills

It's one thing to say you have a certain skill, such as cat wrangling, or press release writing. But it's another thing entirely to have proof that you can do it. For this reason, LinkedIn includes a function that periodically asks your connections to endorse (or virtually recognize) the skills you have listed on your profile. When they do so, they are lending credibility to your claims and helping you enhance your professional reputation. You will receive an email notification whenever a connection endorses you.

LinkedIn will ask you to endorse your connections' skills as well. You can scroll through and react to these suggestions when they pop up. Or, go directly to a profile and scroll down to the *Skills and Endorsements* section and click the plus sign next to the skill you would like to endorse. Because LinkedIn will notify them when you do so, it's a great way to keep yourself top of mind. I have actually received emails from previous clients offering new projects after endorsing them for a skill.

The importance of recommendations

When a potential employer is considering you for a job, they'll usually ask you for references. These are people who can confirm your previous work experience and vouch for your abilities and accomplishments. In a battle between two or more qualified applicants, good references can give you the leg up you need to secure an offer.

LinkedIn recommendations can be seen by your entire network. Much like skill endorsements, recommendations add credibility to your claims and enhance your reputation. But because your connections must do more than click a single box to provide one, recommendations often mean more to recruiters considering you for a job or potential clients vetting your services.

In many cases, you will probably have to request a recommendation from a connection. Consider approaching people who value your work and services, such as previous/current managers and supervisors, previous/current coworkers, industry colleagues, and clients. Doing so is simple:

1. Choose *Privacy and Settings* from the dropdown menu beneath your tiny photo in the LinkedIn toolbar.

2. Look for the link to *Manage your recommendations*.

3. Click the "Ask for recommendations" link at the top of the page.

4. Follow the prompts to complete your request.

Protip: When asking for a recommendation, do not use the generic message LinkedIn generates for you. Instead, enter a custom message for each connection you approach. In the past, I have found customized messages more effective. Not only are they more personal, but they also give you the opportunity to remind your connection about shared experiences. If you are comfortable doing so, you can offer to reciprocate by recommending your connection as well.

What should you list if you are unemployed?

Whether you were laid off or voluntarily left a position, you should still include a current job entry on your LinkedIn profile. Many recruiters search by current job title. If you don't have one listed, they are unlikely to find you.

This doesn't mean you have to lie about your situation. Try one of these approaches instead:

➤ Use the title of the job you want to have and include a phrase such as "in transition" or "ready for new opportunities" in the field for company name. Throw in a few skills as well. This way you will show up in searches, and recruiters can see at a glance that you are looking for your next position. An example: *Project Manager | Construction and Engineering | Currently in Transition*.

➤ Include volunteer work you have done during your job search. While the volunteering experience section of your profile is a natural place for volunteer activities, you can also add them to the job experience section.

➤ Add part-time consulting and freelancing.

Prominently featuring such pursuits makes it easy for recruiters and hiring managers to see that you have continued to hone your skills and practice your trade.

Protip: Don't use words like "unemployed" or "laid off" in your headline, summary, or current job entry. Even if your circumstances are no fault of your own, words like these have negative connotations and are likely to turn off potential employers.

Examples of effective LinkedIn profiles

As the old saying goes, a picture is worth a thousand words. Let's take a brief look at some examples of eye-catching LinkedIn profiles.

Lauren

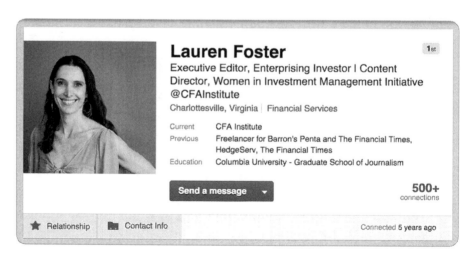

Lauren Foster   1st
Executive Editor, Enterprising Investor | Content Director, Women in Investment Management Initiative @CFAInstitute
Charlottesville, Virginia | Financial Services

Current   CFA Institute
Previous   Freelancer for Barron's Penta and The Financial Times, HedgeServ, The Financial Times
Education   Columbia University - Graduate School of Journalism

Send a message ▼   **500+**
                                                connections

★ Relationship   📇 Contact Info   Connected 5 years ago

With a single glance at Lauren Foster's profile header, we see she is an Executive Editor at Enterprising Investor as well as Content Director at the CFA Institute. She has used a professional-quality photo, which helps her profile stand out in search results, updates, and other parts of LinkedIn. Though she has not customized her LinkedIn URL under *Contact Info*, she has included a website for her employer. She currently has more than 500 connections.

Scroll down and we find her background summary. It is succinct, but is comprehensive enough to paint a picture of her skills and areas of expertise. It is loaded with keywords related to her career (blogging, reporter, editing, digital strategy, communications, etc.).

Background

  Summary

Writer and reporter with more than 20 years of experience, including nine years on staff at The Financial Times.

Currently a content director at CFA Institute, a global, nonprofit organization of investment professionals from over 100 countries worldwide.

Demonstrated professional expertise in the following areas:

- Reporting and Writing
- Blogging
- Newsletters
- Proofreading
- Editing
- Digital strategy
- Twitter
- SEO

Skills: Writing/editing, social media, content curation, content strategy/development.

Follow me on twitter: @laurenfosternyc

She has included her current position as well as past jobs. Each listing includes a summary and links to published content she has created. Some include recommendations from colleagues as well. This is a profile that will not only help build her network, but also may help attract interest from recruiters (even if she has no intention of moving!)

Jason

Jason is a U.S. Coast Guard Officer currently taking part in a fellowship with a Washington, D.C. think tank. Like many military officers, he wears a military uniform in his profile photo when he works in the Coast Guard's command structure, but while he is at the Brookings Institution, he wears formal business attire:

His profile is in excellent shape. His Coast Guard career started 20 years ago, and he has carefully listed his assignments on various vessels and ports, including numbers that help define his responsibilities relating to program management and national security. He might consider breaking them up into easier-to-read bullets, but overall they convey a sense of operational and strategic leadership:

Chief, Prevention Department
Coast Guard Sector San Francisco

July 2011 – July 2014 (3 years 1 month) | San Francisco Bay Area

Led 150-person Department overseeing maritime safety, security and environmental protection operations throughout the greater San Francisco Bay region and Northern California. Oversaw Coast Guard risk management and emergency response activities for 7 commercial ports moving over $70 billion in annual commerce.

Spearheaded deployment of groundbreaking new technologies and infrastructure, including the Nation's first suite of "virtual" Aids to Navigation. Planned and executed North America's first full-scale emergency towing exercise of an Ultra Large Container Vessel (ULCV). Led Coast Guard oversight of the 34th America's Cup on San Francisco Bay in 2013.

U. S. Coast Guard FY2011 Budget Coordinator
Coast Guard Office of Budget & Programs

July 2007 – May 2010 (2 years 11 months) | Washington D.C. Metro Area

Project manager leading development and enactment of Coast Guard's $10 billion annual budget, including all operating funds and $1.4 billion capital investment portfolio for 58,000-person multi-mission armed service.

Led engagement and briefings with DHS, White House OMB, and Congress resulting in enactment of 11 Congressional appropriations.

About the only thing missing from Jason's profile is a summary that ties everything together and gives potential network connections an idea of his strengths and aspirations.

A LinkedIn makeover for Monica

Monica is another professional on LinkedIn who recently updated her profile. The old profile was very basic, and was missing some key elements, such as a photo and custom headline:

Her makeover created a whole new Monica:

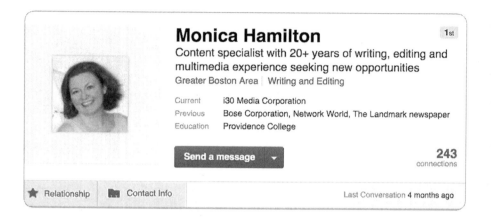

Monica has successfully customized her headline. Her photo makes her appear friendly and engaging. She has even created her own LinkedIn URL.

Monica also improved her summary. This is what it looked like six months ago:

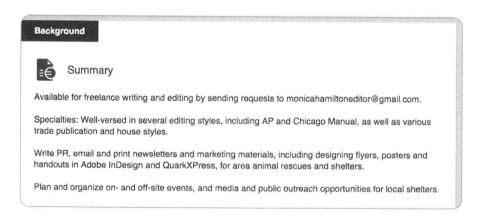

This is what it looks like now:

Background

 Summary

I love working with words. I started my career as a reporter/writer and have expanded my skill set to include content and copy editing as well as page layout, campaign planning and flyer and brochure design. I am looking for more opportunities to bring this combination of skills to new ventures. I am a thorough and meticulous editor with a stellar record of client satisfaction and a dedicated community volunteer with countless hours of professional services donated to worthy causes and nonprofits.

Specialties:
• Well-versed in several editing styles, including AP and Chicago Manual, as well as various trade publication and house styles.

• Vast experience in creating press releases, email and print newsletters, using Constant Contact and iContact, and other marketing materials, including designing flyers, posters and handouts in Adobe InDesign and QuarkXPress, for area nonprofits and animal rescues.

• Years of experience in planning and organizing events, and media and public outreach opportunities for local nonprofit shelters.

Monica's new summary is far more effective than the old one. It gives us a sense of her personality as well as her specialties. We learn *why* she does what she does as well as the services she provides. She has also attached a PDF version of her resume to the summary for interested recruiters and/or potential clients.

Scrolling down, Monica has included her current position as well as four previous jobs. Each one includes a one- or two-sentence summary. All have associated recommendations from colleagues as well. If I were in need of an editor, I would certainly want to learn more about Monica.

Editor
Bose Corporation

June 2005 – June 2015 (10 years 1 month)

Editor of all corporate-produced communications, including press releases, print ads, TV spots, videos, product user guides and technical manuals, store displays and product packaging.

▾ 2 recommendations

 Susan Hamilton
Associate Creative Director at Bose Cor...

If Monica could edit this recommendation, she would. That's because she's been editing my work for years. Her attention to... View ↓

 Brett Cough Perceval
Web Editor at Bose Corporation

Monica is passionate about getting the job done right. She asks tough questions and is very thorough in her work. She has a... View ↓

Senior Copy Editor/Page Designer
Network World

January 2000 – May 2005 (5 years 5 months)

Editor and page designer for technical and feature stories as well as graphics for a weekly tech pub, based outside of Boston.

▾ 2 recommendations

 Gregory Cusack
Experienced Editor & Lifelong Learner

I worked with Monica in the same department at Network World magazine, where I had the pleasure of working on deadline with... View ↓

 Tom Norton
Design Director

I had the pleasure of working with Monica for several years at Network World. Monica's desk handled a lot of content: Daily... View ↓

CHAPTER 4

Networking on LinkedIn

While a comprehensive and well-written profile is essential, even the best profile will generate only limited results if you haven't built a network as well. The connections you make on LinkedIn can lead to skill endorsements, recommendations, and a larger sphere of influence within your industry— all factors that can enhance your professional image. They can also lead to job offers from people in your network, or *their* connections.

As you may recall, LinkedIn's requirements for a "complete" profile include at least 50 connections. Many of the top-performing profiles on the social media site have 500 or more. Of course, before you can start building a network of any size, you have to find other professionals to connect with.

The 4 types of connections

Unlike many other social media networks, which encourage you to "follow" or "friend" anyone and everyone, LinkedIn suggests that its members connect with professionals they actually know. As such, they break down each user's network into four different types of connections.

1st-degree connections are people with whom you are directly connected. You have sent them an invitation and they have accepted, or vice versa.

2nd-degree connections are people with whom you share a mutual connection. You haven't connected directly yet, but you are connected to one or more of the same people.

3rd-degree connections are people who are connected to your 2nd-degree connections.

Group connections are people who belong to the same LinkedIn group as you. Depending on your network, some may also be 1st- 2nd- or 3rd-degree connections.

Protip: The type of connection determines your options for communication. You can contact anyone with a "1st" next to their name through your LinkedIn inbox or by clicking the *Send a message* button on their profile header. If you would like to send a message to someone with a 2nd, 3rd or GROUP designation next to their names, you will need to use InMail. We'll talk more about what InMail is and how to use it later in this chapter. If you don't find any icon next to a LinkedIn member's name, this means they are outside of your network. You must send them a message through InMail if you would like to communicate.

How to find people to connect with

There are numerous ways to find professionals to connect with on LinkedIn. In addition to importing your email address book during the registration process, you can find LinkedIn members to connect with by:

➤ **Visiting the Connections page** by clicking on *My Network > Connections* in the LinkedIn toolbar. LinkedIn will suggest professionals for you to connect with based on your imported email address books, your employer, groups you belong to, and other people in your network.

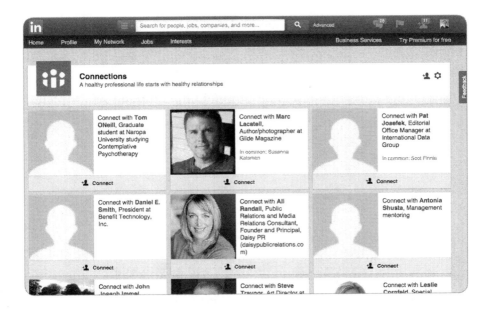

> ➤ **Clicking on *Add Contacts*** in the *My Network* toolbar dropdown menu. LinkedIn will walk you through importing your email address book or books.

> ➤ **Selecting *Find Alumni*** in the *Connections* toolbar dropdown menu. LinkedIn will show you members who attended any university or college during the dates you select.

> ➤ **Using LinkedIn's search feature.** Find the search field in the toolbar, type in a name, click on the magnifying glass icon, and LinkedIn will generate a page of results.

Who should be in your network?

If you are unsure who to add, try searching for the names of current and former colleagues, clients, vendors, and service providers. Classmates, mentors, and people you know from religious, military, or civic organizations are another source of connections. Of course, you can connect with friends and relatives as well—and doing so can help you get your connection count up to the 50 required for a "complete" profile.

However, you should generally have a good reason for asking any LinkedIn member to connect with you, particularly if you have never met or worked together. Maybe you are in the same industry. Perhaps you belong to the same professional organization. You may have interests in common. While LinkedIn allows users to build networks as large as 30,000 people, there is really no need to do so. You will get the most benefit from the social media platform when you target your niche, not when you go after anyone and everyone just to get your numbers up. Note that LinkedIn changes the display to "500+" when your network reaches that level, so you will not get additional public bragging rights if your network grows into the thousands.

Protip: If you send too many invites that are rejected because the member selects "I don't know this person," LinkedIn may suspend your invitation privileges.

Invitation basics

In order to connect directly and establish a 1st-degree connection, one member needs to "invite" the other to connect. Sometimes you will be the one making the effort. At other times, professionals will ask to connect with you. Either way, the process is quite simple.

There are several ways to send an invitation to another LinkedIn member:

➤ Navigate to the member's profile and click the *Connect* button in their header. If they are already a 2nd- or 3rd-degree connection, this button will be visible. If they are outside your network, you may need to click the arrow to the right of the *Send InMail* button and then choose *Connect* from the dropdown menu.

➤ Use the search field in the toolbar to search for a member's name. From the list of search results, click the *Connect* button to the right of the member's information.

➤ Click on *Connections* in the LinkedIn toolbar and import your email address book or scroll through the suggested connections at the top of the page. Click the *Connect* link beneath the member's photo.

➤ When LinkedIn suggests *People you may know* on your homepage, click the *Connect* link beneath a member's photo.

LinkedIn may require you to select from a menu of ways in which you know the person you are inviting to connect. Options include colleague, classmate, friend, business associate, and other. You will usually have the opportunity to personalize the invitation message as well.

Make it personal: Why customized invitations are best

More than once I have received a generic invitation from someone, and have wondered "who is this and how does this person know me?" Often, I will reject such invitations.

But it doesn't have to be this way. It is possible to personalize LinkedIn invitations, which will result in a higher acceptance rate. It's easy to see why.

While the default message LinkedIn generates is rather cold and completely uninformative, a personalized message can be the opposite—especially if you take the time to introduce yourself, mention a mutual contact or shared background, or remind the other member of how you know each other. It can also be helpful to share why you want to connect—whether it's because you admire work they have done or because you would like to get their insight into a prospective employer.

Seriously, when presented with the following invitations, which would you be more likely to accept?

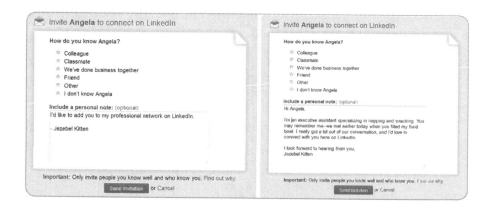

Accepting and rejecting invitations

When another LinkedIn member sends you an invitation to connect, you will receive a notification at the email address connected to your account. The invitation will also show up under the Grow My Network icon (the silhouette on the toolbar).

You can respond to the invitation in several ways:

> ➤ **Click the *Accept* button.** The professional will be added to your network as a 1st-degree connection.

> ➤ **Click the *Ignore* button.** After you click *Ignore*, you also have the option to click I Don't Know [Name]. Doing so will prevent the member

from sending you any more invitations. LinkedIn will also be notified and may restrict the sender's account.

➤ If you have received and ignored multiple invitations from the same person, you may want to click the *Report as SPAM* button. This will be reported to LinkedIn.

Strangers on LinkedIn: Why are they contacting you?

It is not uncommon to receive invitations from LinkedIn members you don't actually know. Who are they, and why are they trying to connect?

Strangers may reach out for a number of reasons. Self-proclaimed "LIONs" (LinkedIn Open Networkers) are relentlessly pursuing a high number of connections and merely want to add you to their score. Others are mining LinkedIn for data to sell to third parties. But it is also possible that the invitation comes from a professional who is legitimately interested in building a relationship. How will you know?

The message that came with the invitation can provide a clue. A generic invitation could be your first indication that it's from someone who doesn't really care about who you are. But before rejecting the invitation, take a moment to look at his or profile. Ask yourself these questions:

➤ **Is the profile complete?** If so, it probably belongs to an active user, rather than someone who is intent on data mining.

➤ **Is he or she in your industry?** If so, you likely share common interests.

➤ **Does he or she belong to the same professional associations or groups as you?** That would also suggest common interests.

➤ **Do you have some of the same connections in common?** If so, their interest in you is likely legitimate.

While I don't blindly accept connection invitations from total strangers, I will make exceptions if I can answer "Yes" to at least two questions in the list above. After all, a larger network can equate to more opportunities.

Reaching out via introductions and InMail

As mentioned earlier, LinkedIn's *Send a message* feature is reserved for communication between 1st-degree connections. But what if you want to send a message to someone who is not a 1st-degree connection? Here are some options:

1. To introduce yourself to a 2nd-degree connection you can use InMail or ask one of your 1st-degree connections for an introduction.

2. If you want to communicate with a 3rd-degree connection or someone outside your network entirely, InMail is your only option.

It's a good idea to request introductions sparingly because it will take your 1st-degree connection time to provide one. If your 1st-degree connection is someone you have never interacted with outside of LinkedIn, you may want to develop your relationship first or you could give the impression that you are more interested in their network than in them. For this reason, I advise against asking a new connection for an introduction until you have liked and commented on several of their updates and posts.

To request an introduction, you will need to do the following:

➤ Navigate to the profile of the 2nd-degree connection you want to be introduced to.

➤ Click the arrow next to the *Connect* button and select *Get Introduced*.

➤ If you have more than one 1st-degree connection who can make the introduction, LinkedIn will ask you to choose one of them.

➤ Next, write a message to the 1st-degree connection who will (hopefully) make the introduction. Let them know why you are making the request.

➤ Finally, click on *Ask for an introduction*.

If an introduction is not possible, you can use InMail to send a message to any LinkedIn member. To use it, you will need to upgrade your LinkedIn account to one of the premium tiers. Premium memberships include Job Seeker Premium, Business Plus, Sales Navigator, and Recruiter Lite.

We'll discuss Job Seeker Premium in a later chapter. If you are on LinkedIn to promote and grow your business, you might consider upgrading to Business Plus. You will get 15 InMail messages and can buy more as needed. As of this writing, it costs $60 per month, but it's possible to try it out with just a 30-day free trial.

Tips for nurturing your network

While seeing your network grow is fun, your connections should be more to you than just a number. Whether they are professionals you know in real life or people you have connected with because you share a common industry or interest, you need to interact with them in positive ways if you want to nurture the relationship. Simple ways to do so include:

➤ Endorsing a skill.

➤ Providing a recommendation.

➤ Congratulating them on a work anniversary or new job (LinkedIn will often suggest this when you visit the site).

➤ Liking or commenting on an update.

➤ Liking or commenting on a post.

Lastly, it is common for 1st-degree connections to ask for help in an update, post, or message. Some requests will be straightforward ("Anyone have a recommendation for a marketing agency in the Chicago area?") while others will require more effort ("I'm changing careers and need a mentor in my new field"). While you may not be able to help every connection who needs assistance, try to make an effort to answer or provide support when possible.

CHAPTER 5

Joining the discussion

When I started freelancing, I had a lot of questions. How should I set my fees? How could I make sure I always got paid? What should I do if I ended up with an impossible client? I spent time Googling these topics, and found a few helpful resources. However, the best answers invariably came from my network of other freelance writers and small business owners. They had dealt with these issues themselves and were happy to share their best practices.

Now that I have established The Quirky Creative and know what I'm doing (at least after I have had my morning cup of tea) I can help out the newbies… on LinkedIn! Doing so not only helps them, it has helped me strengthen connections and establish credibility. You, too, can do the same with updates, posts, and group discussions.

The easiest way to reach out to your network: Updates

To quickly reach out and virtually touch your network, a LinkedIn update is your easiest option. Updates are extremely flexible, allowing you to share anything from images to URLs. The *Share an update* link is prominently situated on your LinkedIn homepage. If you take the strategic approach described below, you should find your update liked, commented on, and re-shared by your 1st-degree connections. This will expand its audience to your 2nd- and 3rd-degree connections as well.

How to share an update

To share an update, complete the following steps:

1. From your homepage, select *Share an update.*

2. Type whatever you would like to say into the "What's on your mind?" field. You can also link to content elsewhere on the Web by pasting in its URL.

3. If you prefer, upload a photo to go with your update by clicking the photo icon.

4. If the visibility of the update is set to *Public*, it will appear within the network feeds of your 1st-degree connections as well as within the feeds of your 2nd- and 3rd-degree connections if a 1st-degree connection likes, comments, or re-shares it. There is also an option to restrict the update to just your 1st-degree connections.

A strategic approach to sharing updates

For the best results, updates should be relevant to your contacts. In other words, they should have some professional context, as opposed to cat photos and other personal updates you might share on Facebook. According to LinkedIn, 60% of members are interested in industry insights, 53% enjoy company news, while 43% want to hear about new products and services.

Here are a few ideas for items you can share with your network:

➤ Links to blog posts or articles you have recently written that might be interesting to professionals in your industry or the industry you would like to be in.

➤ Links to blog posts or articles which others may find helpful.

➤ Inspirational or humorous quotes.

➤ Advice for other professionals in your industry.

➤ Requests for information or advice.

➤ Recent news about your work or your company.

➤ Reminders about deadlines and relevant industry issues.

LinkedIn updates are limited to 300 characters, so choose your words wisely!

Attracting followers with LinkedIn posts

If you have more to convey than 300 characters will allow, you can publish a LinkedIn post. This original content becomes part of your LinkedIn profile and is shared with your connections. It's also searchable both on and off LinkedIn. This means even non-LinkedIn members who search for content related to your topic using Google or another search engine may find your post.

LinkedIn posts also can result in followers. These are LinkedIn members outside of your network who choose to follow what you publish, even if you are not connected. Once they have clicked the *Follow* button next to one of your posts, LinkedIn will notify them whenever you publish a new post. Followers expand your reach significantly without the need to add direct connections.

If LinkedIn's algorithm determines you have published a high-quality post, the site may distribute it beyond your connections and followers on Pulse, LinkedIn's personalized news feed for members. LinkedIn has not revealed how the Pulse algorithm picks content, but there has been speculation that posts doing well within your network of connections and followers (that is, getting lots of likes, comments, and re-shares) are most likely to be featured on Pulse.

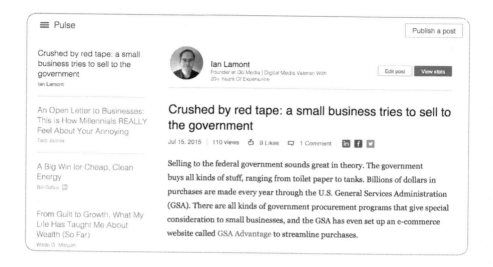

How to publish a post

To get started, simply click the *Publish a post* link in your homepage dashboard. You will then need to complete the following steps:

1. Add a header image by clicking the photo icon at the top of the page. Adding an image will greatly increase the chance of the post being read by others. If you would rather not have a header image, you can remove this box by clicking the "X" in the upper right-hand corner.

2. Enter a headline in the field provided.

3. Type your post into the *Start writing* box. You also can paste content copied from a Microsoft Word or text document.

4. If you would like to create a hyperlink to other Web pages, highlight the text you want to hyperlink and click on the chain icon.

5. You can embed additional images by clicking on the camera icon, or even add video by selecting the icon of an arrow in a circle.

6. Periodically save your creation using the *Save* button. You can also come back to finish the post later.

7. When your post is perfect, click the *Publish* button.

Best practices for posts

Because they become part of your LinkedIn profile, long-form posts should share your professional expertise. You can write about industry trends, solutions you have used to overcome various challenges, tips and tricks of interest to others in your profession, and advice based on your experience. Consider the following best practices for posts your network is certain to notice:

➤ Write a short, concise yet catchy headline that will make professionals want to click through and read the entire post.

➤ Stay focused. Don't try to cover too many topics in one post.

➤ Express your opinion but always remain professional.

➤ Avoid topics that are overtly promotional.

➤ LinkedIn posts do not have word count limits. According to LinkedIn data, the best-performing posts have three or more paragraphs.

➤ Including pictures, videos, and SlideShare presentations increases audience engagement.

➤ Add tags (by clicking the tag icon at the bottom of the post) to make it easier for people searching for information on your topic to find it.

➤ Carefully proofread your post before publishing. Check your spelling in Microsoft Word or another program before posting.

➤ Start discussions with members who comment on your posts. This can help you gain new 1st-degree connections and grow your network.

Making the most of LinkedIn groups

LinkedIn groups are an easy way to meet hundreds of professionals who have the same interests, work in the same industry, and are passionate about the same causes as you. Some LinkedIn groups have tens of thousands of members. When you join a group, all of its members become part of your network (indicated by the *Group* label in search results and elsewhere on LinkedIn).

There's more. Not only can group memberships rapidly expand your network, but they are also additional venues for sharing content, starting discussions, asking questions, posting jobs, and finding job openings. LinkedIn has groups for almost any topic you can imagine, from feline behavior to neurological surgery.

How to find relevant groups

There are several methods you can use to find LinkedIn groups:

➤ **LinkedIn search.** Go to the search field in the toolbar, type in a topic and select *Groups* from the dropdown menu linked to the icon to the left of the search field. Click the magnifying glass icon to the right, and LinkedIn will return a list of group results. For example, there are nearly 300 groups related to microbiology on LinkedIn.

➤ **Discover function.** Choose *Groups* from the dropdown menu beneath *Interests* in the LinkedIn toolbar. Click the *Discover* link to browse a long list of groups algorithmically tailored to your interests.

➤ **Look at the Group section of other members' profiles.** You are likely connected to other professionals who share your interests or industry. Scroll to the bottom of their profiles and check out the groups to which they belong.

How to join a group

LinkedIn groups come in two flavors: *standard* and *unlisted*. Both types have volunteer managers who approve membership, with unlisted groups being invisible to search (you have to be invited to join). There was once another type of group that allowed anyone to join, but these have been discontinued owing to spam and other problems.

To join a group, click the *Join* or *Ask to join* buttons next to the group name. Group managers will review your profile and decide whether to review or decline your application.

Best practices for group participation

LinkedIn will allow you to join up to 50 groups. However, membership is unlikely to benefit you much unless you are an active participant. For this reason, I'd suggest joining no more than 10. Focus on groups that are most relevant to your industry, career, or interests. Avoid those that are not well managed; they tend to be filled with professionals who are only interested in self-promotion. The spam they post adds nothing to the conversation, and can be a distraction if you are notified every time someone adds a new topic.

How you choose to participate in a group is up to you. Options that should yield favorable results (by enhancing your professional reputation, increasing invitations to connect, or catching the attention of potential employers) include:

➤ Regularly participating in discussions.

➤ Answering questions other group members have asked.

➤ Asking thoughtful or stimulating questions of your own.

➤ Posting links to articles other group members will find interesting.

CHAPTER 6

Finding a job on LinkedIn

You have learned how to register for a LinkedIn account, create a profile, make connections, and nurture relationships. We have discussed how doing so can help you establish an online presence and enhance your professional reputation.

But some of you are here for another purpose: You want to use LinkedIn to find your next job. With hundreds of thousands of positions listed on the professional networking platform at any given time, you are likely to find plenty of opportunities.

Before we get into the various ways to find jobs, I want to take a moment to encourage you to complete your profile. If you have not already added the essentials covered in Chapter 3, do it now! While recruiters are searching LinkedIn for qualified professionals, an incomplete or lackluster profile is unlikely to attract much interest.

> **Protip:** Are you employed but thinking about moving on? You can still use LinkedIn for your job search. No one in your network will be able to see the jobs you have searched, viewed, or applied for.

Five ways to find available jobs on LinkedIn

Here are five ways to find available jobs on LinkedIn:

1. **Homepage feed.** Within your network feed, you will find *Jobs you may be interested in.* These positions are recommended by LinkedIn based on information in your profile. If any of your 1st-degree

connections include jobs at their companies in their updates, you will find that information here as well.

2. **Company pages.** There are tens of thousands of company pages on LinkedIn. Most big companies (and many smaller ones, too) list current open positions on their pages. Follow companies that interest you and you will also see the jobs they post in your network feed.

3. **Jobs page.** Click on the *Jobs* link in the toolbar. LinkedIn will take you to your jobs page, where you will find jobs LinkedIn thinks might interest you at the top, and jobs at companies that employ professionals in your network at the bottom. You will need to add your preferences before new listings are displayed.

4. **Groups.** Some groups have a *Jobs* tab that lets members post available positions at their own organizations.

5. **LinkedIn search.** Enter job titles, company names, and other keywords in the search field in the toolbar, and LinkedIn will return relevant search results.

Individual job listings include a description, required skills and experience, and the number of applicants. If you are connected to anyone who works for the organization, LinkedIn will show you who they are and how you are connected on the right-hand side of the page.

LinkedIn will also show you additional jobs. If you look to the right-hand side of the page, you will find jobs viewed by other members. Scroll to the bottom to review similar jobs.

Four tips for using LinkedIn search when looking for jobs

In general, the more keywords or parameters you include in a search, the more targeted—or specific—the returned results will be. This is important when you are searching LinkedIn's impressive database of jobs. To use your time most efficiently, consider these four tips:

1. **Use LinkedIn's advanced search features.** While job title is a good place to start, the nature and level of responsibility in positions with

a particular title will vary by company. Click on the *Advanced* link next to the toolbar search field and filter the results by factors such as experience level, skills, and industry.

2. **Include location as a search term.** If you are not open to relocating for a new job, include location in your advanced search and you will eliminate positions outside your chosen geographic area.

3. **Use "OR" and "AND."** When entering multiple keywords, you can use "OR" and LinkedIn will return jobs with one or more of the words in the posting (for instance, "manager OR director"). Use "AND" and the search results will only return jobs that include *all* of those keywords (for instance, "pediatric AND nurse").

4. **Set up alerts.** When your advanced search yields the results you are looking for, save it by clicking on *Save search* in the upper right-hand corner of the search results page (see image). LinkedIn will then send you an alert whenever new jobs are posted that meet your criteria.

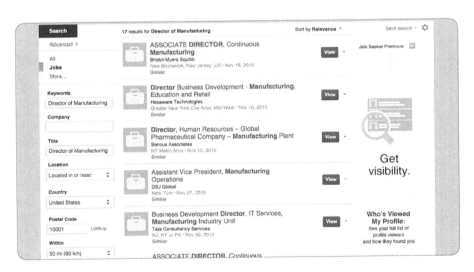

Protip: You can sort job search results by relevance or date posted. As job postings tend to get most of their applications within the first three days, it makes sense to apply for recently posted jobs first before you spend time on those that have been open for a while.

This job sounds perfect! Now what?

You searched for "Cat Wrangler" jobs in the Greater Denver Area and found a position that looks like a perfect fit! There are a couple of ways to proceed:

➤ Click on the *Save* button at the top of the posting page to save the job for later. This is a great option if you are still working on creating your LinkedIn profile or want to research the organization in more detail before you apply. Start the application process by selecting *Apply on company website* or *Apply now*. If the visible option is *Apply now*, you will see a pop-up that allows you to apply for the job with your profile. You can also edit your email address and phone number, and attach a resume and cover letter if you choose.

➤ Sometimes, contacting the employer directly is the best way to get noticed. For this reason, LinkedIn includes the name of the professional who posted the job in the top right-hand corner (unless he or she has chosen to hide this information). If you have a Job Seeker Premium account, you can click on the *Send InMail* button to send a message to the recruiter.

Why some people upgrade to Job Seeker Premium

While finding a job on LinkedIn with a free account is certainly possible, some professionals opt to upgrade to Job Seeker Premium. LinkedIn offers a free 30-day trial, but after the trial is up the service costs $30 per month if you pay on a monthly basis (a discounted rate is available if you pay annually).

The benefits of upgrading include:

➤ A larger profile photo and expanded header, which stand out in LinkedIn search results.

➤ A job seeker badge for your profile header.

➤ Data on everyone who has viewed your profile in the last 90 days—you can reach out and follow up if recruiters or hiring managers check you out.

➤ Up to 10 InMail message each month—use them to contact anyone on LinkedIn!

➤ The ability to narrow search results by salary range.

➤ Salary estimates for jobs posted on LinkedIn.

➤ Insight into how you compare to other professionals who have applied for a particular job.

➤ "Featured Applicant" status—your profile goes to the top of the applicant list.

Four ways to leverage your network when looking for a job

Whether you are trying to attract recruiters, capture the attention of hiring managers, or build relationships with influential professionals in your industry, remember these best practices:

1. **Put those LinkedIn updates to work.** We covered updates in detail in Chapter 5, but there are a few other points to consider when sharing one during your job search.

    First, never write anything that sounds desperate. While you can occasionally remind your network that you are in the market for new opportunities, do not make pleas for help or beg for referrals. Instead, make sure the content you share in your updates engages your audience while furthering your cause.

    For example, you can ask questions about the best skills to develop or certifications to acquire for work in your industry. You can solicit insight on professional organizations and groups. And you can ask your network for their opinions about recent industry-related articles.

    Doing this regularly is important. LinkedIn data shows professionals who share content with their LinkedIn network at least once per week are 10 times more likely to be contacted by a recruiter than those who don't share at all.

2. **Don't be afraid to ask for recommendations.** We talked a bit about recommendations in Chapter 3. They can be especially helpful during your job search. Recruiters and hiring managers *do* read these, so I suggest approaching an assortment of colleagues, supervisors, direct reports and clients who truly know your work. It's even acceptable to offer to draft the recommendation yourself or include a list of the points you would like them to cover in your request.

3. **Use your contacts strategically.** LinkedIn company pages will show you 1st-, 2nd-, and 3rd-degree connections who work at the organization. You can also check out the profile page of the person who posted the job that interests you. On the right-hand side of the profile, you will see how he/she fits into your network. If you have a 1st-degree connection who works at the company or knows the recruiter, you can ask for a referral or a LinkedIn introduction. If your link is a 2nd-degree connection, you can ask a 1st-degree connection for an introduction, then build a relationship and connect with them directly before asking for a referral. Employers like to hire referred applicants. According to Jobvite's 2014 Social Recruiting Survey results, 60% say their best source of job candidates is internal referrals.

4. **Research your interviewers.** Whether you applied for a job on LinkedIn or through another channel, once you have secured an interview, don't forget to use the social media network to learn more about the professional with whom you will be meeting. If his or her profile is comprehensive, you can discover valuable information about that person's career trajectory and time at the company. Working this data into your conversation can make you more memorable when it's time to choose a candidate to hire.

Conclusion

In the past 30 minutes, you have learned how to create a LinkedIn account, optimize your profile, connect with other professionals, leverage LinkedIn groups, and find jobs. You have also learned how to take advantage of other LinkedIn features, ranging from InMail to updates. You know how to publish essays that show off your insights and expertise. You even know how to turn off certain features that might be overwhelming or irritating, such as notifications.

Now it's time to put this knowledge to work. Start by creating or improving your profile, which is the centerpiece of your LinkedIn account and is used by other professionals, recruiters, and employers to evaluate you and make connections. Expand your LinkedIn network by connecting with old colleagues and other people who you have worked with—or want to work with in the future. Join LinkedIn Groups that interest you, or provide additional opportunities to expand your knowledge and professional network. Finally, consider how LinkedIn might help you advance your career, either through a bigger network or increased visibility, or by actively looking for new jobs, companies, or career opportunities.

If you are interested in learning more about LinkedIn, the companion website to LinkedIn In 30 Minutes (*linkedin.in30minutes.com*) includes blog posts, videos, and other information. In addition, please let other people know about this guide, either by leaving an honest review online or telling your personal and professional networks about it.

I have enjoyed sharing my expertise with you, and hope you have gotten a lot out of the guide as well. You can learn more about me at my website, *thequirkycreative.com*, or by looking me up on LinkedIn (*www.linkedin.com/in/thequirkycreative*).

Thanks for reading!

Index

Introduction to
Twitter In 30 Minutes

The following bonus chapter is the introduction to Twitter In 30 Minutes (3rd Edition). To download the ebook or purchase the paperback, visit the book's official website, twitter.in30minutes.com.

One January afternoon, I saw a remarkable event unfold on Twitter.

It was around 3:30 p.m., and I was sitting at my desk. A few people I followed on Twitter suddenly began sending out short text messages (called tweets) about a plane crash. The plane had apparently gone down in New York City, right in the Hudson River. New Yorkers in nearby buildings had seen the crash, or spotted a plane floating in the river, and were sharing scraps of information in the short, 140-character text messages that Twitter allows.

I checked CNN and Google News. There were no official news reports. Yet people on the ground were reporting a disaster. What was going on?

Then I saw someone share the following photograph on Twitter:

The fuzzy photo showed survivors standing on the wing, or stepping into a boat. The tweet that accompanied the photo said:

> *There's a plane in the Hudson. I'm on the ferry going to pick up the people. Crazy.*

I did not know Janis Krums, the person who took the photo from a passing ferry. But the photo and short message he posted on Twitter indicated that many passengers were alive, and were in the process of being rescued. Krums' friends and followers shared the message, which was shared again with thousands of other people. Considering there was no official report or news account of what was happening, it was reassuring to see Krums' tweet.

The story of US Airways Flight 1549 is now well known, thanks to the quick thinking and professionalism of Capt. Chesley B. "Sully" Sullenberger and his crew. More than 150 people were on the plane when it ran into a flock of geese and made an emergency water landing on the Hudson River. It could have been a tragedy. Yet every passenger survived.

But the incident was important for another reason: It showed that Twitter is more than just a collection of fleeting observations about everyday life. Twitter can connect people to events, information, and each other in ways that have never been experienced before.

What is Twitter?

Twitter is a free tool that can connect you with interesting people, events, and information. Twitter is available online at *twitter.com*, or as a free app that can be installed on a mobile phone or tablet. Millions of people all over the world consider Twitter to be as important to their daily communications routines as checking their email, sending text messages, or catching up with friends on Facebook.

How do people use Twitter? Here are some examples:

➤ **Abby** (@AbbyLeighTaylor) is an Oklahoma native now living in Nashville. She loves using Twitter to connect with people who share her interests in music and Mexican food.

➤ **Fiona** (@EmeraldFaerie), a jewelry designer based in London, uses Twitter to show off her latest creations, and let customers know where they can be purchased.

➤ **The New York Public Library** (@nypl) tweets about library programs, author appearances, photographs from its archives, and even job openings.

➤ **Steven** (@IamStevenT) is none other than Steven Tyler, the hard-rock singer and TV personality. On Twitter, he talks about his tour schedule and television appearances, and also uses Twitter to connect with fans.

➤ **Bonnie** (@YourStoryPhotog) is a photographer living in New Hampshire. She likes kayaking, riding her ATV, and sharing beautiful photographs on Twitter.

➤ **Mark** (@mcuban) is a famous entrepreneur who uses Twitter to promote his business interests and basketball team, the Dallas Mavericks. He also answers questions from fans and offers support to people who have seen him on TV or have read his book or blog.

➤ **Socks** (@sockington) is Jason Scott's cat. Like many parody accounts on Twitter, the focus is on humor ("GETTING MY NAILS DONE fine just clawing the couch ..."). Many of Socks' followers are pet owners who have created Twitter accounts for their cats.

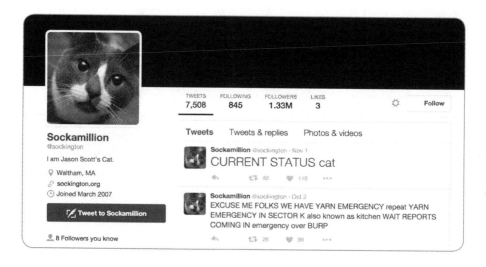

As you can see from these examples, there are all kinds of people, organizations, and interests represented on Twitter. Further, they use Twitter for varied purposes—connecting with like-minded people, promoting their businesses or causes, and having fun.

However, Twitter can be bewildering to newbies. The messages are short. There are strange symbols and unfamiliar conventions. It may not be apparent how Twitter can help you connect with people or start conversations.

The second edition of this guide is intended to help you get your bearings and teach you how to get the most out of Twitter. *Twitter In 30 Minutes* concentrates on core skills and use cases that a beginner should understand. In the next 30 minutes, you'll learn how to do everything from setting up and personalizing your account online or using a mobile phone (Chapter 2), to finding interesting people to follow (Chapter 3). There's a chapter that discusses how to tweet (Chapter 4). You'll even learn a few tricks, ranging from hashtags to retweeting (Chapter 5).

What can Twitter do for you?

At its heart, Twitter lets you do three things:

1. **Broadcast to the world what you are doing, what you are thinking, and who you are with**. The broadcasts are short messages called tweets that contain no more than 140 characters of text. It's also possible to add a photograph or a link to a news story. While anyone can see these tweets, the messages are most likely to be noticed by people who *follow* you on Twitter.

2. **Monitor what other people are saying and doing, and interact with them**. Millions of ordinary people—as well as companies, schools, sports teams, charities, politicians, and superstars—broadcast their own messages to the world. You can choose to follow the accounts of people you like or who you think are interesting. When you follow someone, you will be able to see his or her recent tweets. Some may even follow you back, to see what you have to say, or start conversations with you!

3. **Learn about the world**. Because people all over the world use Twitter to describe what they are doing, how they are feeling, and what they are seeing, Twitter is a window into events, opinions, and information. Want to know what other people think about the latest episode of your favorite TV show or sports team? Want to see photographs taken at a concert, beach, or political rally? Twitter can let you do that. The flow of information is sometimes rough, but it

grants an unfiltered view of the world, often before "official" sources weigh in.

In the following chapters, you'll learn how to follow people, write tweets, and engage in other activities. We only have 30 minutes, so let's get started!

If you're interested in learning more about this title, or buying the ebook or paperback, visit the official website located at twitter.in30minutes.com.

Introduction to Google Drive & Docs In 30 Minutes

The following bonus chapter is the introduction to Google Drive & Docs In 30 Minutes (2nd Edition). To download the ebook or purchase the paperback, visit the book's official website, googledrive.in30minutes.com.

Why you need to use Google's free office suite

Thanks for picking up a copy of *Google Drive & Docs In 30 Minutes,* 2nd Edition. I wrote this unofficial user guide to help people get up to speed with Google's remarkable (and free) online office suite that includes file storage (Google Drive), a word processor (Google Docs), a spreadsheet program (Google Sheets), and a presentation tool (Google Slides).

How do people use these applications? There are many possible uses. Consider these examples:

➤ **A harried product manager needs to work on an important proposal over the weekend.** In the past, she would have dug around in her purse to look for an old USB drive she uses for transferring files. Or, she might have emailed herself an attachment to open at home. Not anymore. Now she saves the Word document and an Excel spreadsheet to Google Drive at the office. Later that evening, on her home PC, she opens her Google Drive folder to access and edit the files. All of her saves are updated to Google Drive. When she returns to work the following Monday, the updated data can be viewed at her workstation.

➤ **The organizer of a family reunion wants to survey 34 cousins about attendance, lodging preferences, and potluck dinner preparation (always a challenge—the Nebraska branch of the family won't eat corn or Garbanzo beans). He emails everyone a link to an online form he created using Google Forms. Relatives open the form on their browsers, and submit their answers. The answers are automatically transferred to Sheets, where the organizer can see the responses and tally the results.**

➤ A small business consultant is helping the owner of Slappy's Canadian Diner (*"We Put The Canadian Back In Bacon"*) **prepare a slideshow for potential franchisees in Ohio**. The consultant and Slappy collaborate using Google Slides, which lets them remotely access the deck and add text, images, and other elements. The consultant shares a link to the slideshow with her consulting partner, so he can periodically review it on the Google Slides app on his phone and check for problems. Later,

Slappy meets his potential franchise operators at a hotel in Cleveland, and uses Google Slides on his iPad to pitch his business.

➤ **An elementary school faculty uses Docs to collaborate on lesson plans.** Each teacher accesses the same document from home or the classroom. Updates are instantly reflected, even when two teachers are simultaneously accessing the same document. Their principal (known as "Skinner" behind his back) is impressed by how quickly the faculty completes the plans, and how well the curriculums are integrated.

➤ At the same school, the 5th-grade teachers **ask their students to submit homework using Docs**. The teachers add corrections and notes, which the students can access at home using a Web browser. It's much more efficient than emailing attachments, and the students don't need to bug their parents to purchase Microsoft Office.

Many people are introduced to Google's online office suite through Docs, the incredibly popular online word processor. Others are attracted by the free storage and syncing features of Google Drive. Microsoft Office, which includes Word, Excel, PowerPoint, and OneDrive, can cost hundreds of dollars. While Drive is not as sophisticated as Microsoft Office, it handles basic documents and spreadsheets very well. Google Drive also offers a slew of powerful online features, including:

➤ The ability to review the history of a specific document, and revert to an earlier version.

➤ Simple Web forms and online surveys which can be produced without programming skills or website hosting arrangements.

➤ Collaboration features that let users work on the same document in real time.

➤ Offline file storage that can be synced to multiple computers.

➤ Automatic notification of the release date of Brad Pitt's next movie.

I'm just kidding about the last item. But Google Drive, Docs, Sheets, Forms, and Slides really can do those other things, and without the help of your company's IT department or the pimply teenager from down the street.

These features are built right into the software, and are ready to use as soon as you've signed up.

Even though the myriad features of Google's office suite may seem overwhelming, this guide makes it easy to get started. *Google Drive & Docs In 30 Minutes* is written in plain English, with lots of step-by-step instructions, screenshots and tips. More resources are available on the companion website to this book, *googledrive.in30minutes.com*. You'll get up to speed in no time.

The second edition of *Google Drive & Docs In 30 Minutes* covers interface improvements that Google rolled out in late 2014 and 2015, as well as the expanded capabilities of the Google Drive, Docs, Sheets, and Slides apps for iOS and Android.

We've only got half an hour, so let's get started. If you are using a PC or laptop, please download the Google Chrome browser, which works best with Google Drive, Docs, Slides, and Sheets. Instructions for the Chromebook and the mobile apps are referenced throughout the guide.

If you're interested in learning more about this title, or buying the ebook or paperback, visit the official website located at googledrive.in30minutes.com.

Introduction to Excel Basics In 30 Minutes

The following bonus chapter is the introduction to Excel Basics In 30 Minutes (2nd Edition). To download the ebook or purchase the paperback, visit the book's official website, excel.in30minutes.com.

Excel:
Not Just For Nerds!

Some years ago, a colleague stopped by my cubicle and asked for help with a project he was working on. John wanted to create a long list of names, categorize them, and assign a score on a scale of one to 10 for each one. He also needed to identify the top scores and create category averages.

John knew I was familiar with all kinds of desktop and online software. He asked, "Which one would you recommend for these types of tasks?"

"That's easy," I answered. "Enter the data into Microsoft Excel or Google Sheets. You can then alphabetize the list, sort by the highest and lowest scores, and draw out category averages. You can even create neat-looking charts based on the results." I used Excel to whip up a basic list, and emailed him the file.

John thanked me profusely, but admitted, "I have only the vaguest idea about Excel and almost no experience with spreadsheets."

John's situation is not unusual. Millions of people know that Excel can be used for financial tracking and number crunching. They may have even opened Excel and entered some numbers into a corporate expense worksheet.

Nevertheless, Excel suffers from an *image problem*. Most people assume that spreadsheet programs such as Excel are intended for accountants, analysts, financiers, scientists, mathematicians, and other geeky types. Creating a spreadsheet, sorting data, using functions, and making charts seems daunting. Many think that these are tasks best left to the nerds.

I'm here to tell you that spreadsheets are not just for nerds. Almost anyone can use Excel for work, school, personal projects and other uses. I've written this guide to help you quickly get up to speed on basic concepts, using plain English, step-by-step instructions, and lots of screenshots. Thirty minutes from now, you'll know how to:

➤ Create a spreadsheet and enter numbers and text into cells.

➤ Perform addition, multiplication, and other simple mathematical functions.

➤ Derive values based on percentages.

➤ Perform timesaving tasks, such as sorting large lists and automatically applying the same formula across a range of values.

➤ Make great-looking charts.

You can imagine how these techniques can help in real-world situations, from tracking household expenses to making sales projections. You can even use them to organize events, and track the office football pool.

We only have 30 minutes, so let's get started!

> *If you're interested in learning more about this title, or buying the ebook or paperback, visit the official website located at excel.in30minutes.com.*

Introduction to Dropbox In 30 Minutes

The following bonus chapter is the introduction to Dropbox In 30 Minutes (2nd Edition). To download the ebook or purchase the paperback, visit the book's official website, dropbox.in30minutes.com.

Got 30 minutes to spare? Good—it's all you'll need to master the basics of Dropbox!

Dropbox is an easy way to store and share photos, documents, spread-sheets, and other types of computer files. Much like the introduction of email, digital photography, and low-rise athletic socks, once you get the hang of Dropbox, you'll wonder how you ever got along without it.

Dropbox works by keeping identical copies of selected files on your computer(s) and Dropbox's cloud-based storage system, and "**automatically synchronizing**" them over an encrypted Internet connection. I've put asterisks around "automatically synchronizing," because this is the killer feature of Dropbox, something that will save lots of time and streamline collaboration. It's cited repeatedly in this guide.

What does Dropbox's automatic syncing feature enable? Here are some common scenarios:

➤ Mark uses Dropbox to **share a folder full of documents with four coworkers,** so they can work on spreadsheets and other documents together.

➤ Jennifer **backs up the photos that she takes on her iPhone, without using cables.** She can immediately access the photos on her laptop.

➤ "Chris instantly backs up the files he's working on in Dropbox. **If his computer crashes or is stolen, he can easily recover them.**

Besides "automatic syncing", another advantage of Dropbox is it follows the same conventions that people already use to save files, create folders, and move stuff around on their computers. This means your Dropbox data will always appear in the familiar "My Computer" (Windows) or Finder (Mac) on your computer. As a result, Dropbox is very easy to learn.

But is Dropbox right for you? Ask yourself if any of the following statements apply to your own technology practices:

➤ You back up files by emailing them to yourself.

➤ You transfer files between two computers using a USB drive.

➤ You want a better way to store and manage digital photos.

➤ You need to collaborate on documents and share files with coworkers.

➤ You're a total klutz who is apt to lose all of the important data on your laptop by dropping it into the swimming pool.

If you found yourself nodding as you read this list, then Dropbox will be an extremely useful utility and time-saver.

Dropbox is also a free service, although heavy users will opt to buy more storage space. But there are several official ways (as well as a few tricks) to get more free storage space, as explained in Chapter 5, "Dropbox—The Rogue FAQ". You'll find many other useful time-saving tips and ways to use Dropbox throughout this guide. The companion website (dropbox. in30minutes.com) contains special features, including videos that demonstrate Dropbox features.

Before we get going, it's good to have a computer handy, or a smartphone, or a tablet. This way, you can quickly try out some the things discussed in this guide. Or you can just read through all of the chapters and install Dropbox later.

Let's get started with Dropbox!

If you're interested in learning more about this title, or buying the ebook or paperback, visit the official website located at dropbox.in30minutes.com.

Notes

Notes

Notes

Notes

Notes

45206485R00059

Made in the USA
San Bernardino, CA
02 February 2017